discovermore

Exploring Primary Sources

Exploring Gutenberg's Bible

Sarah Schmidtt

IN ASSOCIATION WITH

Published in 2025 by Britannica Educational Publishing (a trademark of Encyclopædia Britannica, Inc.) in association with The Rosen Publishing Group, Inc.
2544 Clinton Street, Buffalo, NY 14224

Distributed exclusively by Rosen Publishing.
To see additional Britannica Educational Publishing titles, go to rosenpublishing.com.

Editor: Brianna Propis
Cover Design: Michael Flynn
Interior Design: Rachel Rising

Photo Credits: Cover; (series background) Dai Yim/Shutterstock.com; Cover, p. 24 James Kirkikis/Shutterstock.com; p. 5 Luma creative/Shutterstock.com; pp. 5, 19 Everett Collection/Shutterstock.com; p. 6 AdiDsgn/Shutterstock.com; p. 7 https://commons.wikimedia.org/wiki/File:Diocesan_Museum_in_Pelplin_2019_P01.jpg; p. 8 New Africa/Shutterstock.com; p. 9 https://en.m.wikipedia.org/wiki/File:Boucicaut-Meister.jpg; p. 10 https://commons.wikimedia.org/wiki/File:Morgan_Bible_10r.jpg; p. 11 Ground Picture/Shutterstock.com; p. 12 https://en.m.wikipedia.org/wiki/File:Gutenberg.jpg; p. 13 Sina Ettmer Photography/Shutterstock.com; p. 14 ilolab/Shutterstock.com; p. 15 fatamorgana-999/Shutterstock.com;p. 17 https://commons.wikimedia.org/wiki/File:Ancient_wine_press.jpg; p. 17 Paolo De Gasperis/Shutterstock.com; p. 18 travelview/Shutterstock.com; p. 20 Osugi/Shutterstock.com; p. 21 jcwait/Shutterstock.com; p. 22 3d_man/Shutterstock.com; p. 23 thaisign/Shutterstock.com; p. 25 https://en.m.wikipedia.org/wiki/File:Gutenberg_bible_Old_Testament_Epistle_of_St_Jerome.jpg; p. 26 Kiev.Victor/Shutterstock.com; p. 27 San Hoyano/Shutterstock.com; p. 28 Bushko Oleksandr/Shutterstock.com; p. 29 https://commons.wikimedia.org/wiki/File:Gutenberg_Bible,_on_display_at_the_Library_of_Congress.jpg.

Library of Congress Cataloging-in-Publication Data

Names: Schmidtt, Sarah, author.
Title: Exploring Gutenberg's Bible / Sarah Schmidtt.
Description: Buffalo : Britannica Educational Publishing, 2025. | Series: Discover more : Exploring primary sources | Includes bibliographical references and index.
Identifiers: LCCN 2024030590 | ISBN 9781641903691 (library binding) | ISBN 9781641903684 (paperback) | ISBN 9781641903707 (ebook)
Subjects: LCSH: Gutenberg, Johann, 1397?-1468--Juvenile literature. | Printers--Germany--Biography--Juvenile literature. | Printing--History--Origin and antecedents--Juvenile literature. | Gutenberg Bible--Juvenile literature.
Classification: LCC Z126.Z7 S285 2025 | DDC 686/.1092 [B]--dc23/eng/20240802
LC record available at https://lccn.loc.gov/2024030590t

Manufactured in the United States of America

CPSIA Compliance Information: Batch #CWBRIT25. For further information contact Rosen Publishing at 1-800-237-9932.

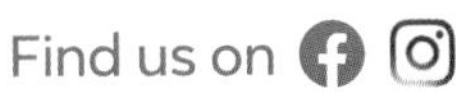

Contents

Firsthand Account

Firsthand accounts of a historical event are known as primary sources. These can include books, news articles, official documents, diaries, photos, and recordings from someone who witnessed the event. They are original sources of information about studied issues, such as the U.S. Constitution or Bill of Rights. A book written about the Constitution or Bill of Rights, however, would be a secondary source. Artifacts can be primary sources as well. Artifacts are objects created by people, and they're important for teaching us about the past. For example, the Gutenberg Bible is one of many copies of the Bible, but it's important because it was the first book to be printed in Europe.

Primary sources are important to understanding history. They provide us with direct information about people, places, and events of the past. They give us historical knowledge that other sources can't. Primary sources allow us to receive a direct glimpse into experiences of the past.

This photograph is a primary source. It shows the National Women's Party protesting outside the White House in 1918.

compare and contrast

Can you think of any primary source examples? How about secondary source examples? What similarities and differences exist between the two?

Most historical books you can find in the library are secondary sources.

Gutenberg's Bible

Many religions have books their followers consider to be sacred. The Bible is an important book to both Jews and Christians. The Bible of Judaism is different from the Bible of Christianity, even though they both include some of the same writings. The Christian Bible is made up of the Old Testament and the New Testament, while the Jewish Bible consists of the Torah, Nevi'im, and Ketuvim.

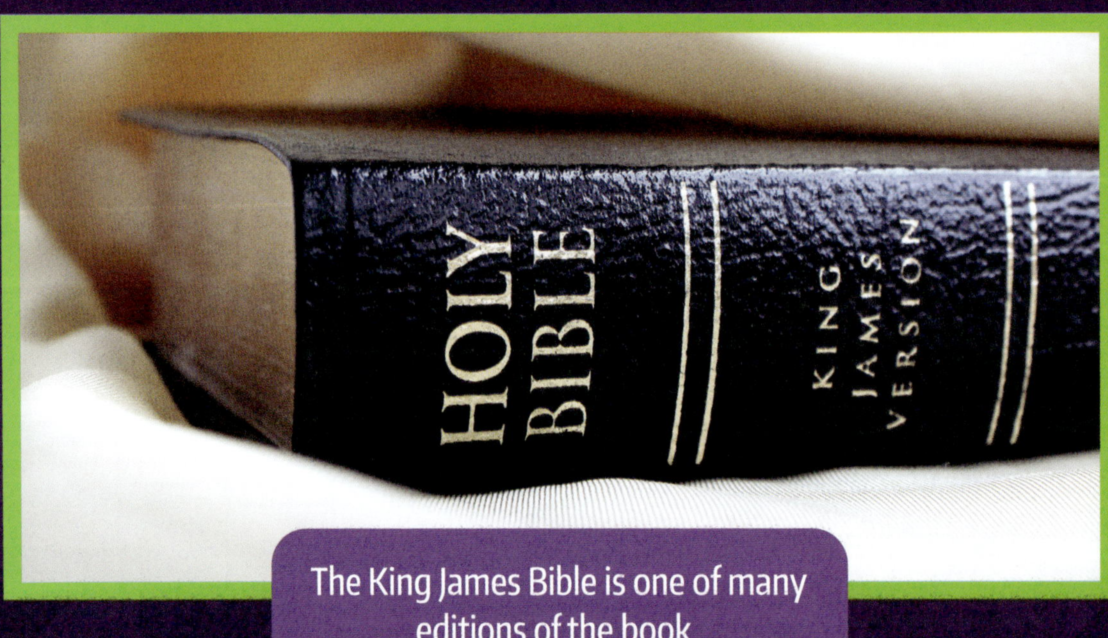

The King James Bible is one of many editions of the book.

The Gutenberg Bible marked the start of the "Gutenberg Revolution" and the age of printed books.

One of the most special copies of the Christian Bible is the Gutenberg Bible. A man named Johannes Gutenberg created it more than 500 years ago. To produce his Bible, he invented a new method of printing. He used movable type and a machine called a printing press. The Gutenberg Bible was the first complete book printed using **movable type** in Europe. It marked the beginning of a revolution in communication and the spread of human knowledge. Today, there are 49 full or incomplete copies of the Gutenberg Bible. These copies are considered among the world's most valuable books.

WORD WISE

MOVABLE TYPE IS A METHOD OF PRINTING THAT ALLOWS PRINTERS TO ARRANGE AND REARRANGE INDIVIDUAL LETTERS—USUALLY MADE OF METAL—TO FORM WORDS.

Bookmaking Before Gutenberg

Before the creation of the printing press, the process of making books was very slow. A single book could take months or even years to finish. This is because each book was copied by hand, a single page at a time. Monks or experienced copyists created most books during this time. They used special pens that needed to be dipped in ink.

Before the invention of the printing press, it would've taken a scribe at least a year to handwrite the Bible.

This illuminated manuscript, known as a book of hours, was created in 1410.

Many of the early books printed in Europe during the 15th century had illustrations. Some of these images were very ornate. Common illustrations included flowers, vines, and religious scenes. In some early books, copyists decorated illustrations with actual silver or gold. These beautiful books are called illuminated manuscripts.

Consider This

Scribes were people who copied documents by hand. How long do you think it would take for you to copy your favorite book by hand?

A Revolutionary Invention

Hand-printed books were very expensive to create since they took months—and sometimes years—to finish. Illuminated manuscripts decorated with gold and silver were even more costly. Only the richest people could afford to own books. Because most people couldn't afford to own books, very few ordinary people learned how to read.

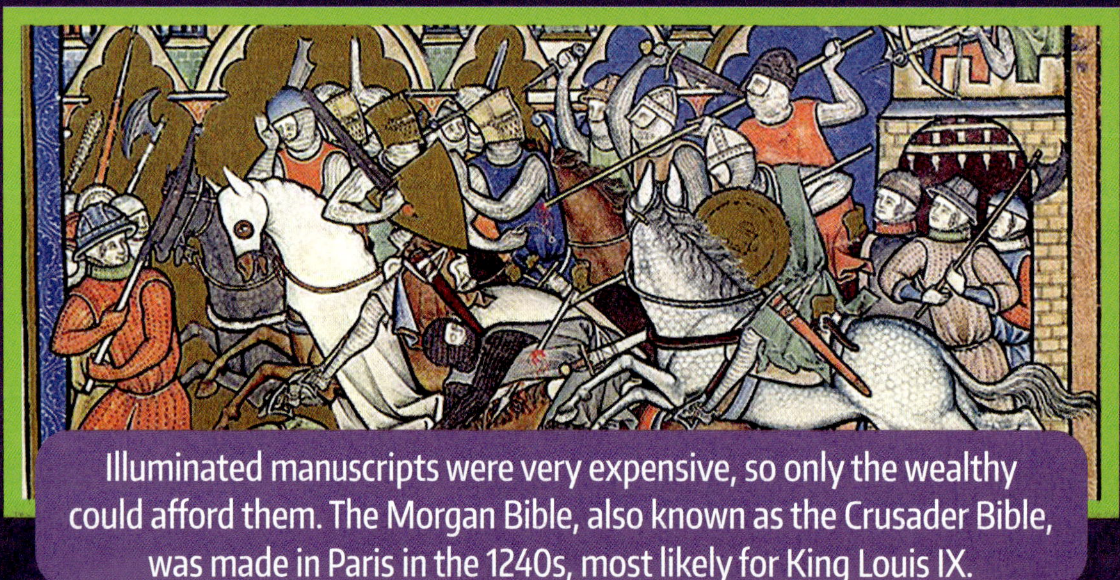

Illuminated manuscripts were very expensive, so only the wealthy could afford them. The Morgan Bible, also known as the Crusader Bible, was made in Paris in the 1240s, most likely for King Louis IX.

The invention of the printing press helped to create a more uniform language and made the prices of books more affordable.

By using movable type and a printing press, Gutenberg could make books much more quickly than monks could by hand. A printing press could produce multiple books in a week. This allowed Gutenberg and others to produce many more books at much lower costs. It also allowed ordinary people to buy books. As a result, **literacy** rates began to rise. Knowledge began to spread rapidly among the masses due to increased literacy.

WORD WISE

LITERACY IS THE ABILITY TO READ AND WRITE.

Who Was Johannes Gutenberg?

Johannes Gutenberg was born in the late 1300s in the Mainz state of the Holy Roman Empire. His father worked as manager at a mint, a place where metal coins are made and stamped with special designs. He was very wealthy. Johannes and his family lived in a large and comfortable house. However, little is known about his actual childhood. We do know that he learned to work with metal at a young age. It's likely that he learned these skills from visiting the mint.

No real pictures of Johannes Gutenberg exist from his time. This is an artist's reimagining of what he probably looked like.

Mainz is in what is now central Germany.

When Johannes was about 13, some residents of Mainz began to fight. Many citizens were angry at families with more money and power, and the Gutenberg family was forced to move away.

Consider This

Johannes Gutenberg developed a system of movable type—made from metal in his adult years. What childhood experiences did he have that could've inspired this creation?

The Birth of the Printing Press

Gutenberg moved from Mainz to Strassburg (now Strasbourg, France) during his young adult life. In Strassburg, he began working in secret on his new printing process. Using his metalworking skills, he experimented with creating small letters out of lead. The individual letters could be arranged to form words and sentences. They could be rearranged later to form different words for different printings.

Strassburg, now Strasbourg, became a French city in 1681.

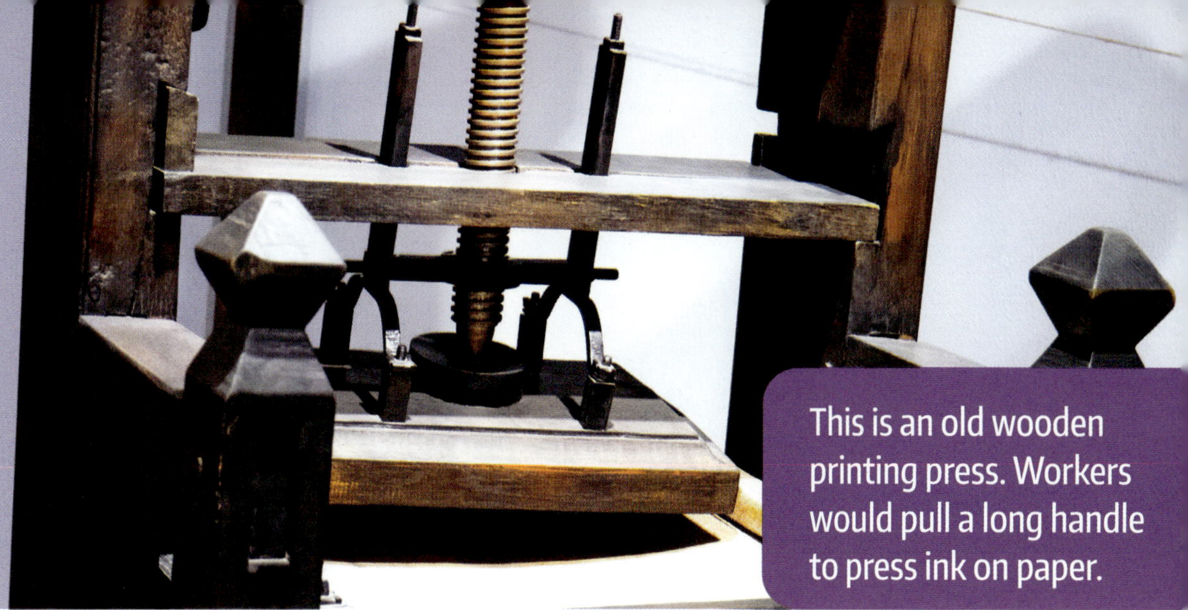

This is an old wooden printing press. Workers would pull a long handle to press ink on paper.

Gutenberg was not the first person to use movable type. However, he also invented a machine that pressed paper against the type. This allowed him to print many words on a page very quickly. During Gutenberg's time, machines existed for pressing grapes into wine, for pressing tree pulp into paper, and for **bookbinding**. To create his new printing press, Gutenberg borrowed designs from these existing machines. His printing process is now considered one of the most revolutionary inventions in the world.

WORD WISE

BOOKBINDING IS THE PROCESS OF BUILDING A BOOK BY BINDING LOOSE PAGES TOGETHER WITH A COVER.

How Did It Work?

One of the first steps in Gutenberg's printing process was to arrange small pieces of metal type. To set type, workers picked out the letters from a case. The case held many copies of every letter in the alphabet. Using these letters, workers spelled out words and sentences. The type was then placed on a flat wooden plate called the lower platen.

After using a roller to spread ink across the type, workers laid a blank sheet of paper on top. They then lowered an upper platen to meet the lower platen. The two plates pushed the paper and inked type together. This action pressed the ink onto the paper. The result was a full page of text, allowing them to print 250 pages per hour this way.

Gutenberg modeled his press after the medieval paper press, which in turn was modeled after the ancient wine and olive presses of the Mediterranean area.

compareandcontrast

Gutenberg's press could print 250 pages per hour. How many pages can a modern computer printer print per hour? How has technology in the printing business improved through the years?

This is a wooden case of metal type. Workers would select which letters they needed, then place them on the lower platen.

Printing the Bible

By 1448, Gutenberg had moved back to his hometown of Mainz. That year his printing press was close to complete. The oldest-known documents believed to be printed by Gutenberg are from around this time. They are a German poem and a document known as Calendar for 1448. Gutenberg continued to improve his printing method but needed many expensive tools. To accomplish his goals, Gutenberg went into business with a rich man named Johann Fust around 1450. Fust gave Gutenberg a large amount of money to help improve his press.

The Gutenberg Museum was founded by a group of Mainz citizens in 1900 to honor Gutenberg's accomplishments. It is in the heart of Mainz, Germany.

This illustration shows Gutenberg (right) looking over a proof, or early draft, with his assistants nearby.

The Gutenberg Bible was printed over the years 1453 to 1455. The new printing press was so effective that the central method was not changed or improved upon for more than 300 years.

Consider This

Gutenberg printed a calendar before printing the Bible. The Bible was his main goal, so why do you think he printed a calendar first?

Laying It Out

The Gutenberg Bible is considered a very beautiful book. However, it was made using a simple design. There were no title pages or page numbers. Each page was arranged with two columns of text. Gutenberg wanted to save paper, so he put many lines of text in each column. Because each column had exactly 42 lines of text, it is often called the 42-line Bible. Each Bible was usually bound into two volumes.

Gutenberg used less paper by arranging the text into two columns on each page.

Around 180 copies of Gutenberg's Bible were printed. 145 of them were printed on paper, and the rest were printed on treated calfskin called vellum.

The paper used to make the Gutenberg Bible was brought over from Italy. Most copies have 1,286 pages. The edges of the paper were a golden color, and the covers were made of leather.

Consider This

It took months for scribes to copy one Bible by hand, whereas Gutenberg and his workers could print multiple Bibles in that same amount of time. Why do you think the printing press became popular?

Metal and Glitter

Most ink was created with water during Gutenberg's time. Water-based inks work well when writing with a pen. Monks had written with water-based ink for hundreds of years. On the other hand, water-based ink did not stick well to Gutenberg's new metal type. The ink would just run off the metal plates. To solve this major problem, Gutenberg invented another important product—oil-based ink.

Today, some companies are using water-based ink once again. It is an eco-friendlier choice because it doesn't use plastic, like other modern inks do.

Oil-based ink, seen here, dries quicker than water-based ink, which meant Gutenberg could also print faster. It looks a lot like paint!

Gutenberg, most likely with some help from painters, made an ink that stuck to the metal type. Oil made the ink much thicker and less runny. It stuck to metal type much better than water-based ink. Gutenberg also added metals such as copper and lead to the ink. This made the surface of the ink glittery. Gutenberg's printing press was made successful—and possible—because of this new ink.

Consider This

After water-based ink didn't work for his printing press, Gutenberg made an oil-based ink to create the Bible. How might painters have been a help to Gutenberg during this process?

Ornamentation

The Gutenberg Bible features mostly black text. When he first began printing, Gutenberg wanted the Bible also to have some red text. To have both black and red text, he had to print each book twice. This made the printing process take twice as long. After some test runs, he decided to print with black ink only.

As seen here, artists added red ink to the black text in the Gutenberg Bible.

paulinum presbiterum de omnibus
divine historie libris·capitulū pmū.
rater ambrosius
tua michi munus-
cula pferens·detulit
sibi et suavissimas
lrās·q̄ a principio
amiciciar̄·fidē pro-
te iam fidei et veteris amicicie no
pferebant. Vera enī illa necessitu
et xp̄i glutino copulata·quā non

Apollonius sive ille magus
loquitur·sive philus·ut pita
dunt·intravit psas·ptransiu
albanos·scithas·massaget
tissima indie regna penetra
extremum latissimo physo
transmisso pvenit ad bragm

Artists painted colorful decorations—called ornamentation—to the pages of the Gutenberg Bible.

Even though Gutenberg printed with only black ink, many copies of the Gutenberg Bible are very colorful. The red ink Gutenberg hoped for was added by hand after printing. The work was done by special artists after Gutenberg and his workers printed the Bible. Along with red ink, the artists added images such as vines, flowers, leaves, and large letters. They used colors such as gold, green, and blue. Many of these images can be seen around the **headings** of every section in his Bible.

WORD WISE

HEADINGS ARE THE TITLES AT THE HEAD OF A PAGE OR A SECTION OF A BOOK.

Fust

Toward the end of the process of printing his Bible, Gutenberg and his business partner, Fust, had an argument. Fust had loaned a large amount of money to Gutenberg to perfect the printing press. Unfortunately, Gutenberg and Fust had different ideas about printing. Fust was a businessman and was interested in making money. He wanted to make Gutenberg produce printed documents much faster. However, Gutenberg was a **craftsman** who wanted his books to be very high quality. He refused to speed up his printing process.

The Gutenberg Monument, built in 1854 in Frankfurt, Germany, features Johannes Gutenberg (left), Johann Fust (middle), and publisher Peter Schöffer (right).

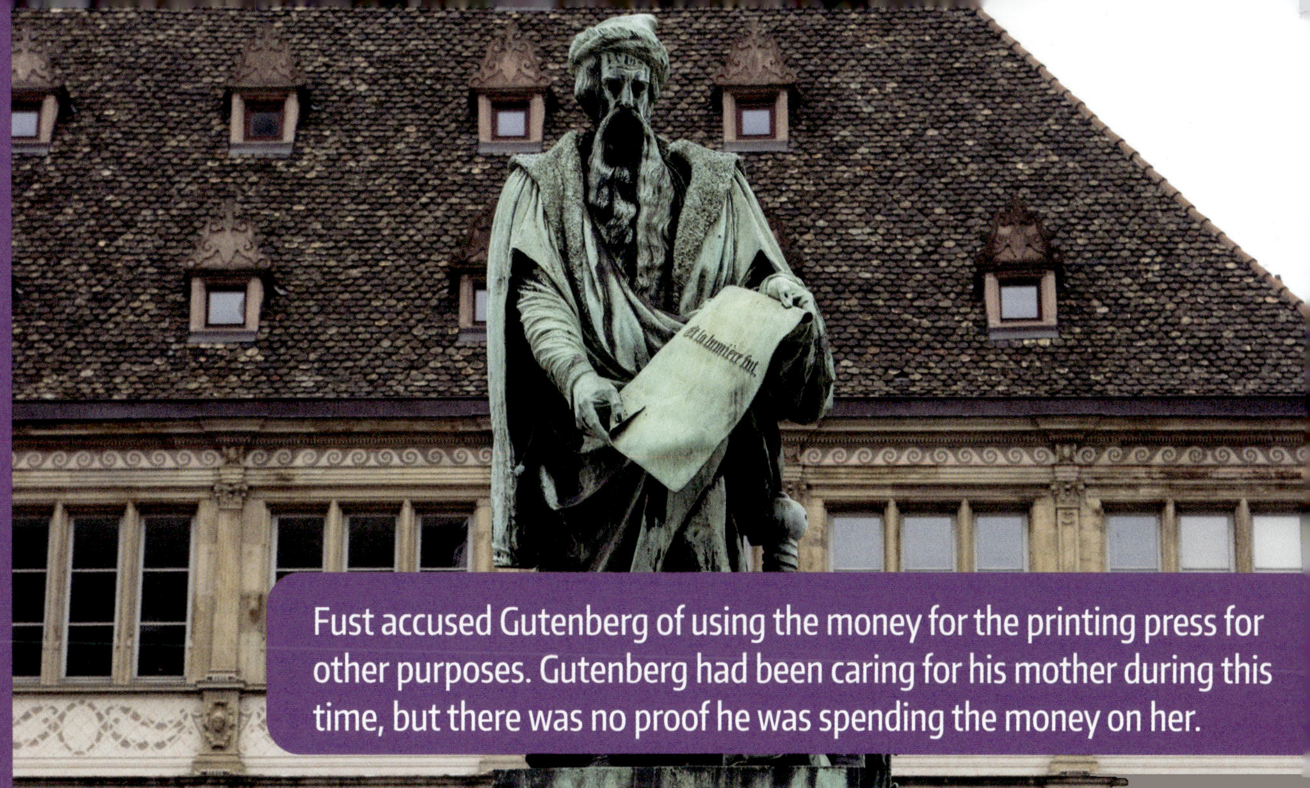

Fust accused Gutenberg of using the money for the printing press for other purposes. Gutenberg had been caring for his mother during this time, but there was no proof he was spending the money on her.

Fust was so angry that he filed a lawsuit against Gutenberg. Fust won the lawsuit. Even though Gutenberg invented the printing press, Fust took over his print shop. Fust and his son-in-law began printing their own books. People once thought the lawsuit ruined Gutenberg's career, but many people now think that he began another successful print shop.

WORD WISE

A CRAFTSMAN IS A PERSON WHO IS HIGHLY SKILLED IN A PARTICULAR CRAFT OR TRADE, SUCH AS PRINTING.

Where Are the Bibles Today?

Fewer than 50 copies of the Gutenberg Bible exist today, despite Gutenberg printing about 180 copies. Some of these copies are unfinished or have been harmed, and several have been dismantled, or taken apart, by booksellers. Booksellers can sell individual pages of the Bible for very high prices. Complete, undamaged copies of the Bible are rare and among the most expensive and sought-after books by collectors in the world. They are worth millions!

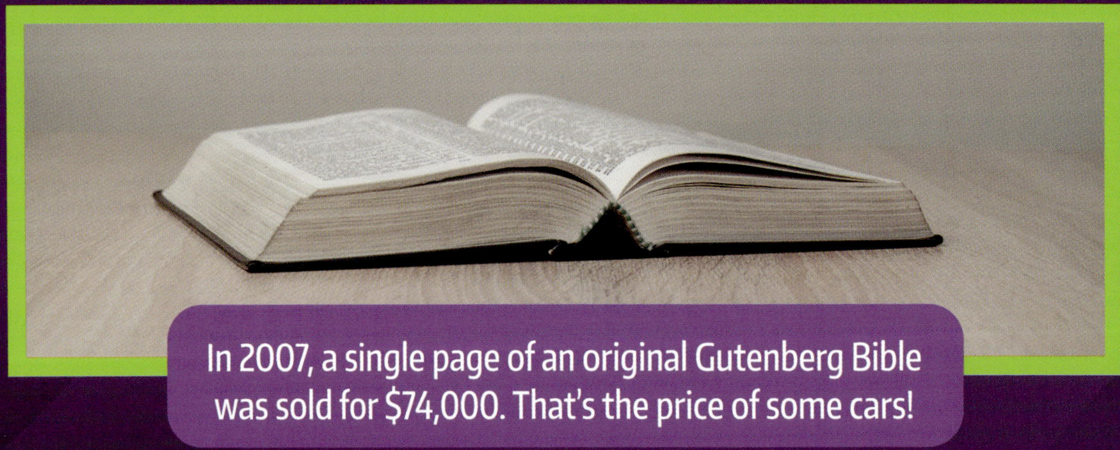

In 2007, a single page of an original Gutenberg Bible was sold for $74,000. That's the price of some cars!

This is the copy of the Gutenberg Bible on display at the Library of Congress in Washington, D.C.

Remaining copies of the Gutenberg Bible are now kept in museums, libraries, or universities. One of the few copies is on display at the New York Public Library in New York City. This copy was shipped to the United States by boat in 1847 and was the first Gutenberg Bible in the United States. Another surviving copy is at the Harry Ransom Center at the University of Texas in Austin, Texas. It's important to keep these copies safe and carefully displayed so people can see these important pieces of history for themselves!

Consider This

Why do you think remaining copies of the Gutenberg Bible are either kept safely at museums and universities or sold for expensive prices? Would this be the case if we had more original copies left?

Glossary

copyist A person who makes copies, especially handwritten ones.
design A plan or model for building something.
document A written or printed paper of information or proof of something.
firsthand Something obtained through someone's personal experience or observation.
information Facts provided or learned about someone or something.
lawsuit A case before a court of law.
lead A soft, bluish-white metal that is easily shaped.
manuscript A written or typewritten book or document.
medieval Having occurred during the Middle Ages, or the period of time between the Roman Empire and the Renaissance.
metalworking The act or process of shaping things out of metal.
mint A place where coins, medals, and tokens are made.
pulp A material prepared chiefly from wood but also from other materials (such as rags) and used in making paper products.
revolution Advancement and change in the way something works or is organized.
technology Applying scientific knowledge for practical purposes, such as the creation of a device.
testament A division of the Bible.
text The main body of printed or written matter on a page.

For More Information

Books

Boone, Mary. *Johannes Gutenberg: Inventor and Craftsman*. Mankato, MN: Capstone, 2018.

Colby, Jennifer. *Printing Press to 3D Printing*. Ann Arbor, MI: Cherry Lake Publishing, 2019.

Murray, Julie. *Printing Press*. Minneapolis, MN: Dash!, 2023.

Websites

Britannica Kids: Johannes Gutenberg
kids.britannica.com/kids/article/Johannes-Gutenberg/353220
Read more about Gutenberg's history and his printing press.

Britannica Kids: Primary Source
kids.britannica.com/kids/article/primary-source/629043#:~:text=A%20 primary%20source%20is%20a,factual%20information%20about%20a%20 subject.
Learn more about what primary sources are and examples of them from history.

Great Innovators: "Gutenberg and the Printing Press" by StoryBots
www.youtube.com/watch?v=DJpJL2YzCOc
Watch a fun video about Gutenberg's creation of the printing press!

Index